Contents

The Journey Through Life

◄ People bring flowers to a Christian funeral. Flowers are a symbol of human life, because they don't last for long.

We are all born as babies and grow up. We get older and at the end of our life, we die. The various religions have ceremonies for burial and cremation that mark the end of people's lives.

Some people believe that there is nothing after death. Yet people of most faiths believe that when they die, their soul – the spiritual part of them – will continue to exist. Their soul will go to a better place, often called heaven, or Paradise. According to some religions, the soul of those who have done bad things will go to hell for punishment. Members of some religions believe in reincarnation. A person's soul is reborn in a new body to live another life. People's beliefs affect the way that they mark the end of life.

SPECIAL
CEREMONIES

Life's End

Cath Senker

SPECIAL CEREMONIES

Life's End

This book is based on the original title *Life's End* by Lynne Broadbent and Denise Chaplin, in the *Ceremonies and Celebrations* series, published in 2000 by Hodder Wayland

This differentiated text version is by Cath Senker, published in Great Britain in 2005 by Hodder Wayland, an imprint of Hodder Children's Books.

This paperback edition published in 2006 by Wayland, an imprint of Hachette Children's Books.

© Copyright 2005 Wayland

Original designer: Katrina Ffiske
Layout for this edition: Jane Hawkins

Consultants:
Working Group on Sikhs and Education (WORKSE);
Jane Clements, The Council of Christians and Jews;
Jonathan Gorsky, The Council of Christians and Jews;
Rasamandala Das;
Dr Fatma Amer, London Central Mosque;
The Clear Vision Trust.

The right of Cath Senker to be indentified as the author of this Work has been asserted by her in accordance with the Copyright, Designs and Patents Act 1988

Wayland
An imprint of Hachette Children's Books
338 Euston Road, London NW1 3BH

All possible care has been taken to trace ownership of each photograph in the book and to obtain copyright permission for its use. If there are any omissions or if any errors have occured they will be corrected in subsequent editions, on notification to the publishers.

Picture acknowledgements:
Circa Picture Library 22, 27; Hutchison Picture Library 16 (J. Horner), 17 (M. MacIntyre); Panos Pictures 5 (S. Sprague), 23 (Jean Léo Dugast), 24 (Jean Léo Dugast); Peter Sanders Picture Library 1 (J. Gulliver), 6, 19 (J. Gulliver), 20 (J. Gulliver), 21 (J. Gulliver); Trip 4 (H. Rogers), 7 (H. Rogers), 8 (P. Rauter), 9 (H. Rogers), 10 (S. Shapiro), 11 (I. Genut), 12 (I. Genut), 13 (H. Rogers), 14 (H. Rogers), 15 (H. Rogers), 18 (Ibrahim), 25 (R. Morgan), 26 (H. Rogers), 27 (H. Rogers), 28 (H. Rogers), 29 (H. Rogers).

British Library Cataloguing in Publication Data
Senker, Cath
Life's End. - Differentiated ed. - (special ceremonies)
1.Death - Religious aspects - Juvenile literature
2.Funeral rites and ceremonies - Juvenile literature
I. Title II.Chaplin, Denise
203.8'8

ISBN-10: 0 7502 4977 3
ISBN-13: 978 0 7502 4977 5

Printed in China

Funerals

Funerals are sad times for friends and family to bury the dead and gather to think about the person who has died. Some faiths try to make funerals a happy celebration of his or her life.

Most faiths have ceremonies to bring together relatives to grieve and support each other. This book looks at how people from the six main religions mark the death of someone from their community.

All religions celebrate the beginning and the end of life with different ceremonies. ▼

The Christian Tradition

Christians believe that Jesus rose from the dead, so death will not be the end for them either. When they die, their soul will have a new life with God. The soul, or spirit, is the special part of a person that makes them who they are.

Christians believe Jesus died on the cross, but rose from the dead two days later. ▼

Preparing to die

Christians who have had disagreements with people try to make their peace with them before they die. Catholics may confess things they have done wrong to a priest. They believe that God will forgive them and their soul will join God in heaven.

Christians see death as both sad and happy. They are sad that they will not see the person again in this life, but happy that he or she has gone on to a better life in heaven.

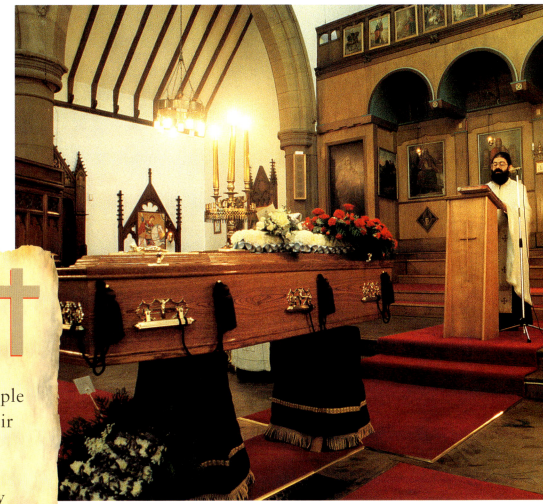

▲ A coffin in church during the funeral service.

SACRED TEXT ✝

This text explains how Jesus came to teach people to be good and save their souls.

'For God...gave his only Son, that whoever believes in Him should...have eternal [everlasting] life. For God sent not his Son into the world to condemn [blame] the world; but that the world through him might be saved.'

The Bible: John 3 verse 16

Returning to Earth

'Earth to Earth, ashes to ashes, dust to dust.' These words are said at most Christian funerals. They remind people of their belief that God made everything. When someone dies, his or her body returns to the Earth.

Some Christians believe that the dead should be buried in a grave. Others prefer to cremate (burn) the body. Usually a funeral director organizes the burial or cremation.

The dead person's body is put in a coffin. Families and friends may come to see the body to say goodbye and to pray for him or her. They may watch over the corpse for the last few hours before the funeral.

Male friends and relatives carry the coffin to the cemetery. ▼

◄ The priest leads prayers at the graveside.

The funeral service

Friends and relatives wear dark clothes to the funeral to show respect. They may send wreaths of flowers. Nowadays, people often prefer to send money to the dead person's favourite charity.

A priest or other religious leader begins the service. Then relatives and friends pray and read from the Bible. They may talk about memories of their loved one.

After the funeral, friends and relatives send cards to the family of the person who has died. Following a cremation, the ashes may be buried, or scattered in the dead person's favourite place.

PAUL'S STORY

'I'm an English Jamaican, and I was in Jamaica when my cousin Martin died. We held a wake – a special party – all night before the funeral. We ate, sang hymns and shared happy memories of Martin.

'At the funeral service, we wore colourful clothes. The coffin was open so we could say goodbye to Martin. We carried the coffin to the grave and sang hymns while we covered it. The funeral was sad but we tried to be cheerful.'

The Jewish Tradition

Jewish people believe that everyone lives just once in this world. Those who are about to die to ask God to forgive the bad things they have done in life. They may say a prayer called the *Shema*, to show devotion to God.

▲ This is a Jewish cemetery.

SACRED TEXT

The beginning of the *Shema*:

'Hear, O Israel,
the Lord is our God,
the Lord is One.
And you shall love the Lord
your God.'

When the person dies, the body is washed and wrapped in a shroud. This is a simple garment made of cotton or linen. A man will be buried with his prayer shawl.

Traditionally, Jewish people are buried, though some may choose to be cremated. The coffin is made from simple wood, to show that in death everyone is equal before God. A close relative stays with the body until the funeral.

The funeral

The funeral is held as soon as possible after the person's death – usually the following day. Jewish people give money to charity rather than bringing flowers. They go to the family's home, where a rabbi leads prayers before the burial. The prayers ask God to help the relatives through their loss and to allow the dead person to rest in peace.

▲ A book of Jewish customs containing a blessing that is often said at funerals.

At the burial, prayers praising God called *psalms* are recited over the coffin. The rabbi or a family member makes a speech about the person who has died. A *psalm* is said as the coffin is placed in the grave, and relatives throw soil onto it.

The *Shiva*

For seven days after the funeral, the family stays at home in mourning. It is called 'sitting *Shiva*' – *Shiva* means 'seven'. During this time they can express their sadness.

While sitting *Shiva*, family members do not wear leather shoes. They may wear a torn item of clothing to show their grief and men do not shave. These are signs that normal life cannot continue while they mourn. Friends come to visit, bringing food so that mourners will not have to prepare meals themselves.

Each day a service is held. *Kaddish*, the mourning prayer is recited. It reminds people of the greatness of God even at times of sadness.

▲ These men are sharing the mourner's sadness during the *shiva* period.

Anniversaries

At some time after the *shiva*, a gravestone is placed over the grave. A service marks the occasion. This year and on every anniversary, the family will light a special candle to remember their loved one.

▲ A *yahrzeit* candle, which burns for 25 hours, is lit on the anniversary of the death.

Naming babies

It is traditional to name babies after people in the family who have died. This helps to keep memories of them alive.

Beliefs about the next world

Some Jews believe there will be a Day of Judgement when God will bring back the dead and judge their deeds. Yet they believe that the most important thing is to follow God's Commandments (laws) during their lives. They should focus on leading a good life on Earth rather than preparing for the next world.

SIMON'S STORY

'I'm 14 years old, and recently my grandfather died. As soon as mum told me, we went straight to my grandmother's house, where the family was gathered.

'The following day was the funeral. Some of the mourners tore their jackets to show their sadness. The rabbi was kind to us because he knew we were upset. As he prayed I remembered my grandfather's face, which somehow made me feel better.'

The Hindu Tradition

▲ Shiva, a deity representing one aspect of God.

Hindu beliefs

Hindus believe that life is like a circle, just like the seasons. People are born, they die, and are born again. Each person may have thousands of lives. Hindus believe that when they die, their *atman* (soul) passes into another body. This is called reincarnation.

Most Hindus want the circle of birth and death to end so they will be reunited with Brahman, the Supreme Spirit. The result of their actions in life is called *karma*. If they are good and have good *karma* they will eventually be liberated from the circle of birth and death.

SACRED TEXT

This sacred text explains reincarnation.
'Just as the dweller in this body passed through childhood, youth and old age, so at death he similarly passes into another body.'

Bhagavad-gita: Chapter 2, Verse 13

▲ The body is covered with flowers and taken to the funeral pyre.

Cremation

In India, when people die they are cremated, usually on the same day. The body is washed, with water from the holy River Ganges if possible. Sweet-smelling sandalwood paste is rubbed over it and copper coins are placed over the eyes.

The body is wrapped in a white cloth and taken to the funeral pyre. A son of the dead person walks around the pyre and sets fire to the wood. A priest chants verses, often from the holy book, the *Bhagavad-gita*. Hindus believe that as the body burns, the *atman* is able to leave the previous life and move on to the next life and the next body.

RANJEE'S STORY

'I live in Ontario, Canada. Two years ago, my aunt died and the whole family came for the cremation.

'On the day, a Hindu priest came to our house to chant verses from the *Gita*. One said: "As a person takes off old clothes and puts on new ones, so the *atman* leaves one body and enters a new one." That summer we went to India to scatter my aunt's ashes over the River Ganges.'

Three days later, the eldest or youngest son collects the ashes of the body and scatters them over a river. Hindus try to scatter ashes over the River Ganges because they believe it can wash away the dead person's *karma*.

Many Hindus build funeral pyres near the River Ganges. ▼

▲ Hindus gathering to mourn a community member.

After the funeral, the family members mourn for 10 days. Friends and relatives visit each day, bringing them food. During this time, the mourners eat no sweet foods and men do not shave. These are signs of grief and respect for the departed soul. People offer special foods, such as rice balls and milk, to the family shrine. On the twelfth day, friends and family enjoy a special feast.

The Muslim Tradition

The journey of life

When a baby is born, the call to prayer is whispered into its ear. The prayers that normally follow it are not said. They are said in the mosque when that person dies. For Muslims, life is a journey that ends with death.

When Muslims are dying, they try to say the *Shahadah*, the statement of faith in Allah. They believe they will be with Allah after death.

▲ Muslims may visit the graveside of a loved one regularly.

SACRED TEXT

Muslims believe that good people will go to Paradise:
'People who have faith and do righteous [good] deeds are the best of creatures. Their reward is with Allah: they will live for ever in Gardens of Eternity...'

From the *Qur'an: Surah* 98: 7–8

Islam teaches people to accept that death is part of Allah's will. They read the *Qur'an* regularly for three to seven days after the death of a loved one. It contains comforting words. Friends and relatives offer food and comfort too.

Preparing for burial

Muslims bury their dead because Allah said that fire should not be used to destroy what he has made. The body is prepared for burial by a close friend or relative of the same sex.

Muslims saying prayers at a graveside in Granada, Spain. ▶

Everyone is treated equally when they die. The body is dressed in plain clothes. These often include the robes that the person wore on pilgrimage to the holy city of Makkah in Saudi Arabia.

The burial is arranged quickly – within 24 hours if possible. There are prayers at the mosque, led by close male relatives or friends.

The burial

The dead person is buried lying on his or her right side, facing Makkah as Muslims do in prayer. The grave is built up with soil to show that this is a special place. At festivals, Muslims often visit graves to show respect for their dead.

▲ This Turkish-Muslim picture shows angels.

The Day of Judgement

Muslims believe that two angels watch over them, recording their good and bad actions. They know they must behave well to reach Paradise.

Muslims believe the souls of the dead wait to go to Paradise. This will happen on the Day of Judgement. On this day, the universe will be destroyed and the dead will rise again. The angels will give Allah the records of everyone's behaviour. He will decide who will enter Paradise. The good people will live there forever in great happiness. Bad people will be sent to hell. Those who believe in Allah but have sinned will go to hell for a short while and then enter Paradise.

◀ Muslims believe Paradise has fountains, as this garden does.

MARYAM'S STORY

'I live in Cairo, Egypt. My mum died last autumn and I was very upset. My aunt and some women friends prepared her body for burial. They dressed her in plain clothes.

'The following day in the mosque, I watched the funeral prayers from the women's gallery. I miss mum terribly but if it is Allah's will, we'll meet again in Paradise.'

The Buddhist Tradition

Buddhist beliefs about death

Buddhists believe that birth and death are a natural part of life. As a young prince, the Buddha was out in the town one day when he saw an old person, a sick person and a dead body. He realized that unless people understood that nothing lasts, they could never be truly happy. They needed to understand that things are always changing, and accept it.

Different beliefs

The ceremonies that take place when a Buddhist dies depend on the traditions of the country. Buddhists in different countries have different ways of marking death.

The Buddha died surrounded by his friends and followers. ▼

When someone dies, his or her family and friends feel sadness and grief. However, Buddhists try to remember that death is a natural change. They may see the body of the person who has died. It reminds them that they too will die one day.

▲ This funeral service is in South Korea, Asia.

Life after death

The teaching of karma says that the way you behave affects your future. Buddhists believe that after they die they will be reborn into another life. If they are kind, they will be happy in this new life and in the ones to come. But if they are greedy and selfish, they will be unhappy in their future lives.

Some Buddhists believe that it is important for dying people to be reminded of the Buddha's teaching by reading sacred texts. If they are too ill to do this, their friends or Buddhist monks will recite them.

SACRED TEXT

'Whatever living beings there be – feeble or strong, long, stout or medium, short, small or large...those who are born and those who are to be born – may all beings, without exception, be happy.'

From the *Meditation on Loving Kindness, Metta Sutta*

▲ These monks are making offerings to the Buddha during a funeral.

Preparing the body

After death, the body is washed. It is put in a coffin or wrapped in material, with candles, flowers and incense around it. The funeral does not take place straight away, to give people from far away time to get there. During that time, monks may come to the house to chant from the Buddhist holy scriptures. Some Buddhists take the coffin to the temple and take turns to sit and meditate around it.

The funeral ceremonies

In parts of Asia, the ceremonies last for over 49 days – the first seven are the most important. Prayers are said every seven days for seven weeks. Western families tend to have prayers said less often.

The funeral

Most Buddhists are cremated. The night before, people often gather to eat and play music. On the funeral day, they accompany the coffin to the crematorium, carrying flowers and incense. Monks may walk alongside, chanting *sutras*. The coffin is burnt on a funeral pyre and the ashes are collected.

In Tibet, the body is left on a mountain to feed hungry vultures. Buddhists believe this is a way of being generous with something you don't need anymore.

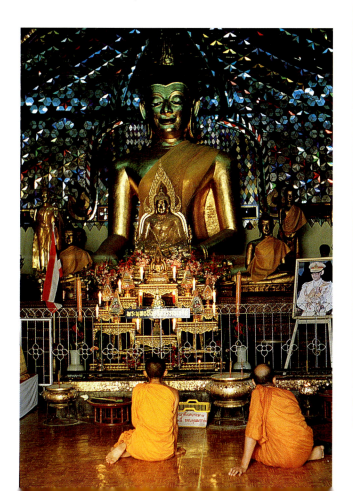

SHANTI'S STORY

'I live in Cambridge, England. When my grandfather died, his body was taken to the shrine room in the temple. It stayed there for two days, surrounded by flowers and images of the Buddha. Many friends and relatives came to pay their respects.

'On the day of the cremation, we went to the crematorium. We repeated Buddhist sayings because the Buddha's teachings help us at sad times like this. Others in our Buddhist community, the *sangha*, were a comfort to us too. A few days after the cremation, we went to the shrine room again to meditate.'

◀ After a funeral, people meditate at a shrine to the Buddha.

The Sikh Tradition

The cycle of birth and death

Many Sikhs believe in reincarnation. In each life, the soul learns new lessons and becomes closer to God. Finally, when all the lessons have been learned, the soul will be freed from the cycle of birth and death and will join God. The way to achieve this freedom is to be guided by God and perform good deeds. Sikhs try to avoid the bad things in life.

Friends and family visiting a dead person before the funeral. ▶

▲ A *granthi* reads from the *Guru Granth Sahib* at a Sikh funeral.

When a Sikh dies

At the death of a Sikh, evening prayer is said and everyone says '*Waheguru*!', which means 'Wonderful Lord'. Everyone is treated equally in Sikhism, so funerals are the same for rich and poor alike. Sikhs believe in cremation. The body is no longer important because the soul will move to another one. The cremation takes place on the day of death, or the following day.

First, the body is washed. Traditionally, yoghurt and water are used. The body is dressed in new clothes and the Five Ks, the symbols of the Sikh faith. It is brought home for people to pay their last respects before the funeral. Family and friends arrange for the Sikh holy book, the *Guru Granth Sahib*, to be read.

▲ This is a Sikh cremation service.

The funeral

Before the cremation, the body is brought to the *gurdwara*, the Sikh place of worship. Prayers are said outside the building. A procession takes the body to the cremation site.

At the site, family and friends say a prayer over the coffin. The eldest son or a close relation lights the funeral pyre. Then everyone returns to the *gurdwara* for a religious service with *shabads*, Sikh hymns.

Everybody has *karah parshad* (a special sweet), and shares a meal called *langar*. The ritual of sharing reminds Sikhs that everyone is equal and that life must go on.

RUPINDER'S STORY

'I was on holiday in India when my aunt died so we went to the funeral. A huge procession of people walked through the streets of the town carrying her body, which was covered with a white cloth.

'At the *gurdwara*, we stopped for prayers, then continued to the cremation site. There were sweet-smelling woods and incense on the funeral platform. We said prayers and sang hymns as the body was cremated. Everyone said how much they'd miss my aunt.'

After the cremation

Friends visit the family during the next two weeks to provide support and help around the home. Sikhs believe that death is not sad. It means that the person has moved closer to God.

Scattering the ashes

Many families arrange for the ashes of the dead person to be taken to Kiratpur, near Anandpur Sahib in India. They are sprinkled on to the flowing waters of a river. Sikhs that cannot get to India arrange to sprinkle the ashes on to the nearest river or sea.

Sikh women preparing *langar* to eat after the funeral of a member of their community. ▶

Glossary

Allah the Muslim name for God.

Bhagavad-gita the Hindu sacred text that was spoken by Krishna, one of the many forms of God.

cemetery a place where dead bodies are buried.

cremation the burning of a dead body.

crematorium a place where dead bodies are burned.

Five Ks the five symbols of Sikhism, which begin with 'K' in Punjabi: shorts, uncut hair, sword, bracelet and comb.

funeral pyre a pile of wood for burning a dead body.

granthi a reader of the Sikh holy book, the *Guru Granth Sahib*.

Guru (Buddhism, Hinduism and Sikhism) a teacher.

incense a substance that is burned to give off a pleasant smell.

karma (Buddhism and Hinduism) the teaching that actions affect your life and future lives; also means the results of actions.

mourn to feel and show sadness because someone has died.

Paradise (Islam) the place where good Muslims will go to be with Allah after the Day of Judgement.

pilgrimage a journey made for religious reasons.

priest (in various religions) a person who performs religious ceremonies.

Qur'an The holy book of the Muslims.

rabbi (Judaism) a teacher.

reincarnation (Hinduism, Sikhism) the rebirth of a soul into a new life.

shrine room (Buddhism) a place where people come to worship, which usually has an image of the Buddha.

soul the spiritual part of a person that is usually seen as eternal.

sutra words from the Buddha.

wreath an arrangement of flowers, usually in a circle, placed on a grave to show respect.

Books to Read

Beliefs and Cultures: Buddhist; Christian; Hindu; Jewish; Muslim, Watts, 2003.

Celebrations and Rituals: End-of-life Rituals by Matilde Bardi et al., Cherrytree Books, 2003.

Life Times: Journey's End by Anita Ganeri, Evans Brothers, 2004.

Our Culture: Buddhist; Hindu; Jewish; Muslim; Sikh, Watts, 2003.

Rites of Passage: Funerals by Mandy Ross, Heinemann, 2004.

A World of Festivals: Family Festivals by Jean Coppendale, Chrysalis Children's Book, 2005.

A Year of Religious Festivals series: *My Buddhist Year; My Christian Year; My Hindu Year; My Jewish Year; My Muslim Year; My Sikh Year* by Cath Senker (Hodder Wayland, 2004/2005)

Index

All the numbers in **bold** refer to photographs